Author:

Alex Woolf studied history at Essex University, England. He is the author of over sixty books for children, many of them on historical topics. They include *Days That Shook the World: Assassination in Sarajevo* and *Past in Pictures: A Photographic View of World War One.*

Artist:

David Antram was born in Brighton, England, in 1958. He studied at Eastbourne College of Art and then worked in advertising for 15 years before becoming a full-time artist. He has illustrated many children's non-fiction books.

Series creator:

David Salariya was born in Dundee, Scotland. He has illustrated a wide range of books and has created and designed many new series for publishers in the UK and overseas. David established The Salariya Book Company in 1989. He lives in Brighton with his wife, illustrator Shirley Willis, and their son Jonathan.

Editor: Victoria England

Editorial Assistant: Mark Williams

Published in Great Britain in MMXIV by
Book House, an imprint of
The Salariya Book Company Ltd
25 Marlborough Place, Brighton BN1 1UB
www.salariya.com
www.book-house.co.uk

PB ISBN-13: 978-1-909645-22-6

SALARIYA

1 3 5 7 9 8 6 4 2

A CIP catalogue record for this book is available from the British Library.

Printed and bound in Singapore.

Visit our website at **www.book-house.co.uk**
or go to **www.salariya.com** for **free** electronic versions of:
You Wouldn't Want to be an Egyptian Mummy!
You Wouldn't Want to be a Roman Gladiator!
You Wouldn't Want to be a Polar Explorer!
You Wouldn't Want to sail on a 19th-Century Whaling Ship!

Visit
www.salariya.com
for our online catalogue and **free**
interactive web books.

PAPER FROM
SUSTAINABLE
FORESTS

You Wouldn't Want to Be in the Trenches in World War One!

Written by
Alex Woolf

Illustrated by
David Antram

A hole you'd rather not be in

Created and designed by
David Salariya

BOOK HOUSE
a SALARIYA *imprint*

Contents

Introduction

It's August 1914. You are 16-year-old Tommy Atkins, living in London. War has just broken out in Europe. The Allies, led by Britain, France and Russia, are fighting the Central Powers, led by Germany.

You're very proud of your country. Britain is the most the powerful nation in the world, with an enormous global empire. But recently, Germany's grown powerful, too, and is now challenging Britain for the role of top superpower. In Britain, everyone is very enthusiastic about the war and confident of victory. You get swept up in the excitement. Many people optimistically predict a victory by Christmas. Little do they know that because of new weapons and tactics the conflict will drag on for four years and will be one of the bloodiest, most gruesome wars ever fought.

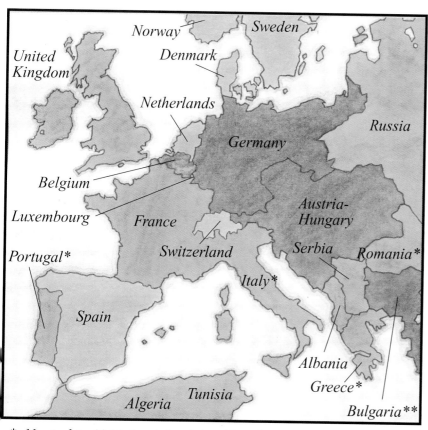

Allies

Central Powers

Neutral countries

* Neutral in 1914, but joined the Allies later in the war
** Neutral in 1914, but joined the Central Powers in 1915

Joining up

Even though you're under age, you join the queue at the local recruiting centre and try to enlist with the army. When it's your turn to be interviewed, the recruiting sergeant asks for your age. You tell him and he says 'Clear off, son. You can't join up unless you're 18 and can't fight until you're 19. Come back tomorrow and see if you're the right age.' So you return the next day and give your age as 19. Then you hold up your right hand and swear to fight for king and country. The sergeant winks and hands over your first day's wages. You realise that the army is so desperate for soldiers, it's prepared to bend its own rules.

FIGHTING PHYSIQUE. You can't join up unless you're at least 5 foot 6 inches with a chest size of 35 inches.

YOUR COUNTRY NEEDS YOU. Lord Kitchener's impressive moustache and pointing finger are responsible for recruiting millions.

TAKING THE OATH. Recruits have to swear loyalty to king and country.

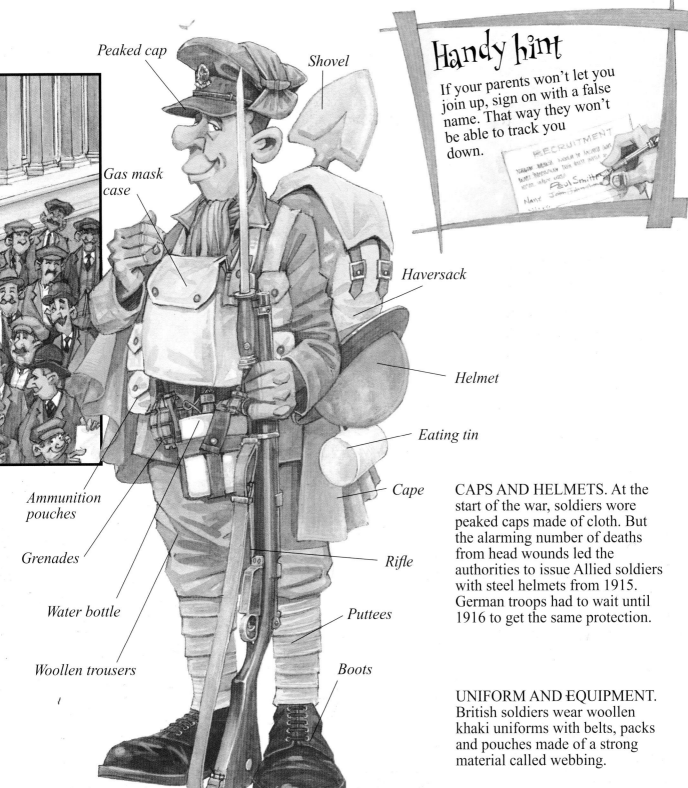

Peaked cap

Shovel

Handy hint

If your parents won't let you join up, sign on with a false name. That way they won't be able to track you down.

RECRUITMENT

Paul Smith

Name   John Johnson

Gas mask case

Haversack

Helmet

Eating tin

Ammunition pouches

Cape

CAPS AND HELMETS. At the start of the war, soldiers wore peaked caps made of cloth. But the alarming number of deaths from head wounds led the authorities to issue Allied soldiers with steel helmets from 1915. German troops had to wait until 1916 to get the same protection.

Grenades

Water bottle

Rifle

Woollen trousers

Puttees

Boots

UNIFORM AND EQUIPMENT. British soldiers wear woollen khaki uniforms with belts, packs and pouches made of a strong material called webbing.

Training

Y ou're sent to your regimental depot where you receive your kit, then to a training camp to join your battalion. Here you get your first taste of army discipline and training. You sleep in a tent because there aren't enough huts. There are shortages of kit and equipment, and for the first few days you train in your own shoes and a red jacket dating back to the Boer War. There's also a shortage of officers because all the experienced ones are in France, fighting. Men have been brought out of retirement to train recruits. One gives out instructions while sitting in a Bath chair.

Right, I've taken this pin thing out, now what do I do?

Aaaarghhh!!!

NEW SKILLS. You're given training in physical fitness, how to march, first aid and how to defend yourself against a gas attack.

You're also taught basic field skills, like how to handle your weapons safely, fire a gun, throw a grenade and fight with a bayonet.

TO FRANCE. After just a few weeks' training, you're sent to a camp in northern France. You see the wounded returning from the front.

Handy hint

The French call bayonets 'toothpicks', but don't be tempted to use them for that purpose!

I fought in the Crimea, don't you know.

Bath chair

The trenches

You go 'up the line' to the trenches. The trench at the front is the 'fire trench' and behind that are rows of support and reserve trenches where you can fall back if under attack. Beyond the fire trench is 'No-man's-land', then the German trenches. These lines of opposing trenches stretch all the way from the North Sea to Switzerland. You quickly learn that life in the trenches can be both tough and boring. Every day begins with a 'stand-to' an hour before dawn, when the enemy is most likely to attack: every man has to stand on the trench fire step for an hour or more, rifle loaded, bayonet fixed.

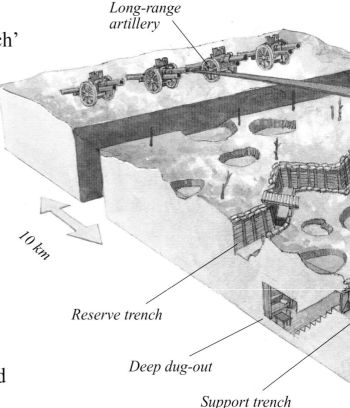

STAND-TO. Tommies dread this daily routine. They call it 'Morning Hate'.

Long-range artillery

10 km

Reserve trench

Deep dug-out

Support trench

Front-line dug-out

GERMAN TRENCHES (left) are the best: deep and lined with concrete, with dug-outs 15 m below ground, safe from shell fire.

BORING DAYS. When not on sentry duty or digging, soldiers retire to their dug-outs. They fill their idle moments writing letters, playing cards or singing songs.

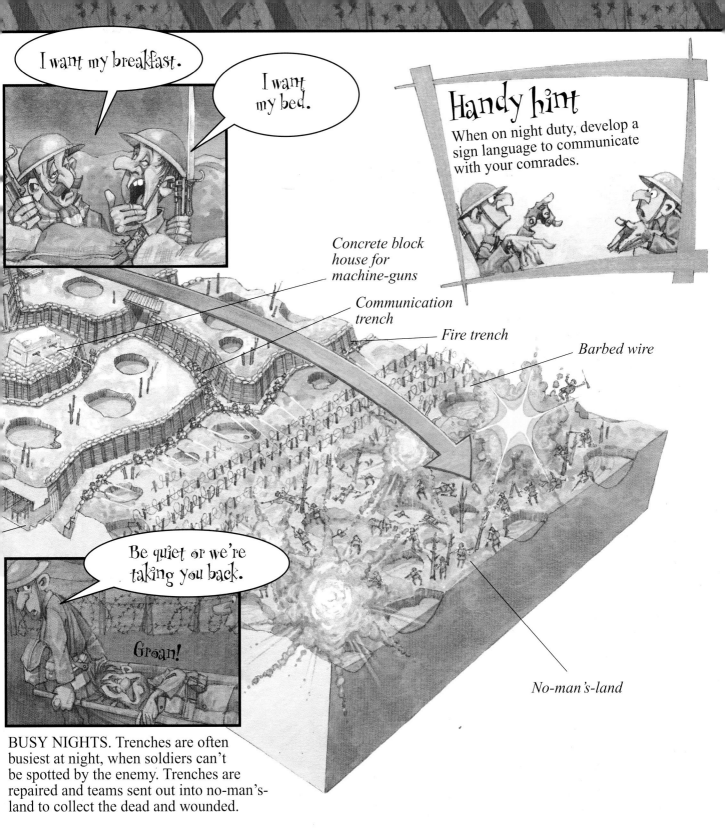

I want my breakfast.

I want my bed.

Handy hint

When on night duty, develop a sign language to communicate with your comrades.

Concrete block house for machine-guns

Communication trench

Fire trench

Barbed wire

Be quiet or we're taking you back.

Groan!

No-man's-land

BUSY NIGHTS. Trenches are often busiest at night, when soldiers can't be spotted by the enemy. Trenches are repaired and teams sent out into no-man's-land to collect the dead and wounded.

Rats and lice

You are forced to share your trench with some quite unpleasant creatures, including frogs, horned beetles and fat red slugs. Worst of all are the rats and lice.

RATS GET FAT. The rats eat your rations and spread disease among your comrades. Some grow as large as cats by eating unburied corpses. They show no fear of you and crawl all over you while you sleep…

Yuck!

I must say, the German rations are far tastier!

RAT-A-TAT-TAT. Soldiers fight back by shooting the rats. If the sergeant catches them, they'll be put on a charge for wasting ammo. Sometimes men bait the ends of their rifles with bacon to get a shot at close quarters.

Hands up, you dirty rat!

Handy hint

If the rats have been at your bread, place the loaf on the floor, then turn out the light. When you hear them, switch on your torch and attack!

HIGH-TAILING IT. Many veterans swear that the rats can sense impending enemy shellfire and flee the trenches hours before it begins, just as their sea-based cousins might desert a sinking ship.

OF LICE AND MEN. Lice are another annoying trench pest. They itch like crazy, leave red blotches on the victim's body and spread diseases such as trench fever and typhus.

CHATTING. Lice hunting is called 'chatting'. Soldiers kill lice by running a thumbnail – or sometimes a lit candle – up the seams of their shirts and trousers, where the lice are most deeply entrenched.

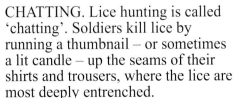

13

Bully beef, bread and biscuits

Your daily ration of food is pretty awful. It's mainly bully beef (canned corned beef), maconochie (a stew of meat, turnips and carrots) and bread. You also get biscuits and jam. The jam is almost always plum and apple.

MAKING DO. By 1916, flour is in such short supply that bread is made from ground turnips, sometimes with added sawdust. Meat may be horse or dog. 'Vegetable' soups and stews are made with weeds and nettles picked from nearby fields.

Have you finished your horse stew?

There's still a bit between my teeth.

Yum, tea-flavoured soup!

FOUL FLAVOURS. The British kitchen staff prepare all the food in the same large vats. As a result, everything tastes of something else.

Handy hint

If you'd rather not risk your teeth on the biscuits, they do make excellent firelighters!

HARD BISCUITS. It takes up to eight days for bread to reach the front line, so it's always stale. The biscuits are so hard, soldiers often soak them in water for a few days, then heat and drain them and add some condensed milk. The resulting mush is said to be quite edible.

COOL CUISINE. By the time food reaches the front line it's always cold. Sometimes a group of soldiers manage to obtain a cooking stove so they can heat their food and brew some tea.

The cold and the wet

Autumn turns to winter with no sign of an end to the war. There is constant rain. Trenches become rivers and frequently collapse. The rains have caused the latrines to overflow into the trenches, spreading disease. Some soldiers prefer to risk death by sleeping outside the trenches.

When on sentry duty, you're forced to stand in a freezing, waterlogged trench for hours on end without being able to remove your wet socks or boots. Your feet have gone numb and the skin is turning blue. You have trench foot! Luckily for you, it's treated before it goes gangrenous. Otherwise it might have had to be amputated.

CHANGE YOUR SOCKS. Soldiers can avoid trench foot by drying their feet and changing their socks at least twice a day. But that's easier said than done in a waterlogged trench!

Is that you, Briggs?

WATER WATER EVERYWHERE. Many British trenches are in damp, low-lying ground. Life is a constant battle against water and mud.

DYSENTERY is a problem because of the lack of proper sanitation. Also, drinking water is often in short supply, so soldiers must depend on impure water collected from shell-holes.

FROSTBITE can be a real hazard in winter. Soldiers are advised to strip off and smear their bodies in animal fat for insulation.

Under fire

About ten million tonnes of artillery shells are fired against enemy positions during the Great War. Shelling is constant, reaching its greatest intensity before an attack. After several weeks at the front, the never-ending *boom-boom-boom* is starting to fray your nerves. You feel tired and irritable and get frequent headaches. One of your comrades becomes so distressed that he deliberately wounds himself so that he can go to hospital.

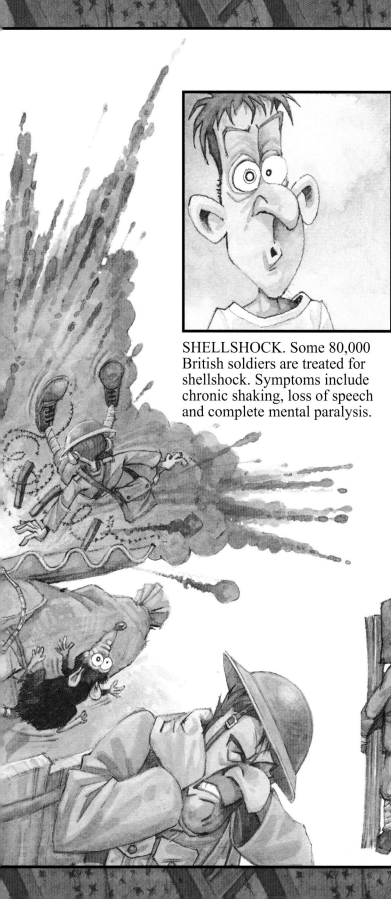

If you're an officer who has to punish a troublemaker, make him scrub your dug-out floor with a toothbrush.

SHELLSHOCK. Some 80,000 British soldiers are treated for shellshock. Symptoms include chronic shaking, loss of speech and complete mental paralysis.

Self-inflicted, was it?

BLIGHTY WOUNDS. Some wound themselves in order to escape from the front line. Those found guilty of this may be executed.

DEATH PENALTY. Soldiers accused of cowardice, running away, disobedience, throwing down arms or falling asleep on sentry duty are given a court martial (a military trial). If found guilty, they are often shot.

19

No-man's-land

You are selected as part of a patrol to venture into no-man's-land to discover information about the enemy. You must take control of a shell-hole in front of the enemy trench so you can spy on them. Your patrol goes out at night, crawling forward on your stomachs, faces blackened with burnt cork, trying to avoid getting caught in barbed wire. The Germans send up a flare and fire on your patrol. You dive for cover into the shell-hole and then must spend hours lying there silently in the mud, pretending to be dead.

NIGHT RAIDS. Men are often sent into no-man's-land at night on spying missions or to capture enemy soldiers for interrogation.

LIGHT FLARES. To stop British night patrols, the Germans use light-shell rockets. The flare blazes brightly for up to a minute, giving defending troops a chance to fire at the patrol.

Hang on, is this wire ours or theirs?

Handy hint

If sent on a night raid, take silent weapons such as knives, clubs, knuckledusters and hatchets.

BARBED WIRE is placed in front of trenches to foil enemy infantry attacks. Night parties are sent out to repair these defences or cut the enemy's wire.

Animals of war

Your platoon has received its very own dog, a terrier called Jim. He was sent from a special training school in Scotland and is proving a fine rat-catcher and a reliable messenger. He's small, fast and can move over any terrain to deliver messages. He's also helped lay a telephone cable and has been trained to give early warning of a gas attack, as he will smell it before humans do. Jim's arrival has provided a much-needed morale boost for the men.

So what's the latest from the front?

We're running low on dog biscuits, sir.

DOGS. As well as delivering messages to and from the front, dogs can find wounded soldiers and can carry a first-aid package strapped to their throat.

Handy hint

The best way to stop a carrier pigeon delivering its message is to send out a squadron of hawks!

CHER AMI was a famous carrier pigeon, which delivered its message despite receiving wounds to its leg and eye. Over 100,000 carrier pigeons are used in the war, and more than nine out of ten reach their destination.

It's not exactly the Charge of the Light Brigade, is it?

HORSES. Machine-guns and trenches mean there is no place for cavalry charges in modern warfare, but horses and mules are invaluable for transporting materials to the front.

ELEPHANTS are used by the Germans for transporting supplies in occupied France.

Tanks, tunnelling and other terrifying tactics

In their desperation to break the deadlock on the Western Front, military leaders on both sides turn to new methods. In September 1916, you see huge, strange-looking machines trundling slowly towards the German front lines – it's your first sighting of tanks, and they terrify you and your comrades as much as they do the Germans. You learn later that for those driving the tanks, the experience isn't exactly pleasant either. Tanks are hot and noisy inside and, since they lack springs, the crew are thrown around like peas in a can. But on the right terrain they prove very effective at breaking through German lines.

METAL MONSTERS. The first British Mark I tanks are slow, cumbersome and often break down.

I think you may need to get out and push.

Handy hint

To detect enemy tunnelling, drive a stick into the ground and hold the other end between teeth to feel any vibrations.

AIRCRAFT are crude and unreliable. Pilots fly in cramped cockpits and there is no room for a parachute.

Time to bale out. Now where's my...? Oh.

CREEPING BARRAGE. With this tactic (below), introduced in 1916, artillery fire moves forward in stages, just ahead of advancing infantry. The timing has to be just right to avoid killing friendly soldiers.

SUBTERRANEAN SABOTEURS. Miners are employed to dig tunnels under no-man's-land and place mines beneath enemy trenches.

GAS ATTACK! You see a yellow-green cloud drifting towards you. Get your gas mask on quick! Chlorine gas causes a slow death by suffocation.

Over the top!

I t is now June 1917. Your squadron is to be part of a major British Army offensive at Messines. An offensive is a large-scale attack on enemy lines using at least a corps (up to 45,000 soldiers). You are excited, nervous and very scared. The battle starts at 4.30 a.m. with an enormous bang. The earth shakes as 600 tonnes of explosive previously laid by miners are detonated under German lines, opening up enormous craters. You wait nervously on the fire step. The whistle blows and you go over the top. Under a creeping barrage of heavy artillery you advance on the enemy trenches. Machine-gun fire cuts down comrades on both sides. You keep going . . .

Hooray! We've advanced five miles!

Yes, but what are we going to do for food?

OFFENSIVES usually require sustained fighting in advanced positions, making it difficult to supply the attacking army with food, ammunition and other essentials.

Charge!

Handy hint

A 1915 British Army handbook suggests fixing a broken limb with a splint made from a rifle or a roll of newspapers.

WOUNDED. During the assault, you get shot. You dive into a shell-hole and use your field dressing to treat your wound.

STRETCHER-BEARERS. With just four stretcher-bearers per company, you must wait several hours before you are rescued.

CASUALTY CLEARING STATION. After your wound has been cleaned, surgery is carried out to remove the bullet.

Back to Blighty

You are sent back to England with other soldiers wounded in the battle. You travel by ship across the Channel, then by train to London where an ambulance picks you up and delivers you to the military hospital.

The ambulance moves at walking pace to avoid jarring, as many of the soldiers are badly wounded. Children run along beside the ambulance, cheering. You feel like a returning hero. There are so many casualties from the front that the staff at the hospital are almost overwhelmed.

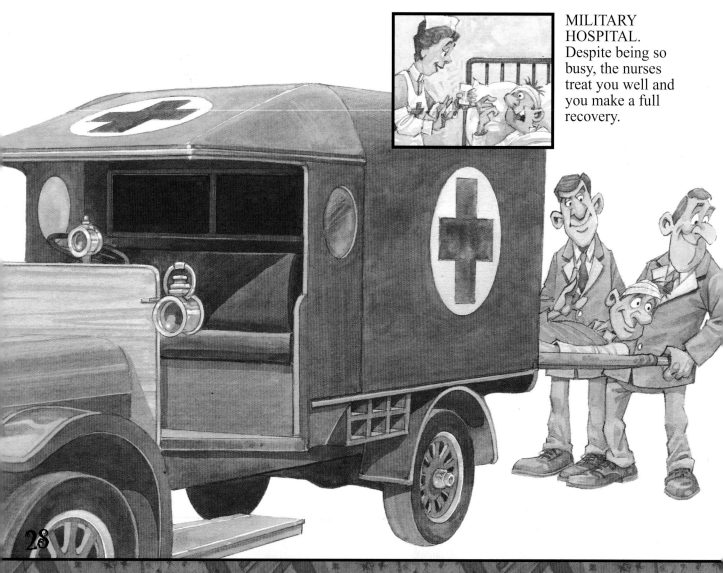

MILITARY HOSPITAL. Despite being so busy, the nurses treat you well and you make a full recovery.

HOME AGAIN. Because you were under age when the war started, you are not sent back to the front. You go home and are reunited with your family.

MUM AND DAD have spent the war helping to make shells at a munitions factory. Like millions of other women, it's the first job your mum's had.

Handy hint
Don't bother trying to talk about your experiences to those who weren't there. Few will want to hear about it. But don't worry: future generations will come to appreciate the horrors of the War in the Trenches.

ARMISTICE. On 11 November 1918, the Germans agree to stop fighting and an Armistice is signed. The war is over!

REMEMBRANCE. You join in the street celebrations . . . but you also feel sad for all the friends you have lost.

Come on, tell us all about it.

Bang! Bang!

Glossary

Armistice An agreement made by opposing sides in a war to stop fighting for a certain time.

Artillery Large guns used in warfare on land.

Bath chair A large, old-fashioned wheelchair for the disabled.

Battalion A large body of troops ready for battle.

Bayonet A sword-like stabbing blade fixed to the muzzle of a rifle.

Blighty A slang term for Great Britain used by British troops serving abroad. A 'Blighty wound' is a wound serious enough for a soldier to be sent home.

Block house A reinforced concrete shelter.

Boer War Either of two wars fought by Britain in South Africa in 1880–1881 and 1899–1902.

Chlorine gas A greenish-yellow, poisonous gas used as a weapon.

Company A group of soldiers consisting of several platoons, commanded by a captain or a major.

Corps A subdivision of an armed force in the field, consisting of two or more divisions.

Court martial A court for trying soldiers accused of offences against military law.

Dug-out A shelter dug in the ground and roofed over.

Dysentery Infection of the intestines causing severe diarrhoea.

Field dressing A bandage carried by soldiers for immediate use in case of gunshot wounds. It consists of a large pad of absorbent cloth attached to a strip of fabric to bind the pad in place.

Fire step A step on which soldiers in a trench stand to fire.

Gangrenous Suffering from gangrene, which is the death and decomposition of tissues in a part of the body.

Great War The name by which World War One was usually known at the time.

Infantry Foot soldiers.

Khaki A dull brownish-yellow colour used for uniforms by armies worldwide.

Kitchener, Lord Secretary of State for War at the start of World War One.

Latrine A communal toilet.

Munitions Military weapons, ammunition and equipment.

Neutral Not taking sides in a conflict.

No-man's-land The area between the front lines of two opposing armies.

Platoon A group of soldiers commanded by a lieutenant.

Puttees Long strips of cloth wound around the lower legs for protection.

Rations An amount of food supplied on a regular basis to members of the armed forces during a war.

Regimental depot A place where supplies such as equipment and food belonging to a regiment (a permanent unit of an army) are stored.

Sentry duty A period during which a soldier is stationed to keep guard or to control access to a place.

Shell-hole A crater made by a shell (an explosive artillery projectile or bomb).

Shellshock A psychological disorder caused by prolonged exposure to shellfire.

Shrapnel Sharp fragments of metal from an exploded shell or bomb.

Splint A strip of rigid material used for supporting a broken bone.

Tommy Nickname given to British soldiers in World War One – short for Tommy Atkins.

Western Front The zone of fighting in western Europe during World War One, involving the German, French, British and (after 1917) US armies.

Index